INTIMACY
✍ *with the* ✍
DIVINE

Rev. Sr. Freda Ehimuan

FOREWORDED BY JULIET EHIMUAN CHIAZOR

WESTBOW°
PRESS
A DIVISION OF THOMAS NELSON
& ZONDERVAN

WestBow Press books may be ordered through booksellers or by contacting:

WestBow Press
A Division of Thomas Nelson & Zondervan
1663 Liberty Drive
Bloomington, IN 47403
www.westbowpress.com
1 (866) 928-1240

ISBN: 978-1-4908-2691-2 (sc)

Printed in the United States of America.

Library of Congress Control Number: 2014903039

WestBow Press rev. date: 5/21/2014

PASSIONATE ENCOUNTER WITH THE DIVINE

Where goes love when lovers caress
Rolling in seasons while boundary sway
I am the lover sealed by timeless sway
The wind of silence the kiss of passion
The rain a fondle that ripples the heart
The stroke of love channels the heart

To my dearest and beloved Sister, Mrs Juliet Ehimuan Chiazor
for her encouragement, love and faith which inspired
the publishing of this journal. May the love of God
that burst forth in creation fill you with Joy.

ᥕ INTIMACY WITH THE DIVINE ᥕ

These pages will profitably provide the reader with ample opportunity to share a unique and personal experience of the divine from the treasured memoirs of the author. Her personal experience is encapsulated in a rare flow of poetic expressions; since poetry dialogues with human psyche in a manner that is deep and refreshing. It gives the author a privileged opportunity to convey things spiritual with anecdotes that are customary to the mystics. God willing; I am confident that these experiences are bound to be helpful even to the unspiritual way farer in his/her desire to establish an encounter with the divine. There is no doubt that these stories and encounter with the Lord present unique lessons from a *"favoured walk with the Lord"* in the garden of life. Although they do not seem to be too farfetched from common daily experiences; yet these experiences offer depths that resonate with mystical meanings that point the way to encounter with God even in secular or mundane environments. Your reading of these pages would perhaps reveal that you have not sufficiently treasured the moments that are often gratuitously offered you with a touch of the divine as you unknowingly traverse the world of nature in your daily walk through life. As we surf freely on the waters of life. We are reminded that the world of nature offers boundless opportunities of encounter with the divine especially, if we paused to invite God's hand to guide the dance of the soul with Him in the lonely and unfamiliar quiet world that lies beyond words and sight. Wander and contemplation are necessary doors to access this awe inspiring world that lies beneath the distraction waves of our noisy existence.

Indeed, one is bound to feel guilty for not taking the occasion to stand and stare so as to recognize and dialogue with God's inviting and loving presence in the world of nature. The privileged experience of the author's encounter with the diving should fill us with a deep sense of loss and remorse as we recall how we usually fall prey to the distraction of our noisy existence which often fails to satisfy our deepest yearnings. As a result we are often left in greater emptiness with a wounded and spiritually starved preoccupation as these distracting moments fade quickly like the morning dew.

As I read through these pages it is like I got invited to pounder Is. 55: 1-2 "Oh, come to the water all you who are thirsty; though you have no money, come! Buy and eat; come, buy wine and milk without money, free! Why spend money on what cannot nourish and your wages on what fails to satisfy? Listen carefully to me, and you will have good things to eat and rich food to enjoy".

It is a wise counsel and warning that in modern times unless one takes a personal walk with the divine one runs and risk of sinking fast into an abysmal shipwreck from the avalanche of heresies and half-truths that we perpetually face in our empty and noisy world. A personal encounter with the divine seems to point to the truth of this counsel that each one of us is to search for God ten times as earnestly as possible. Thankfully, we are not to look for miraculous thunderbolts from on high before knowing that all the fleeting moments we are privileged to pass through are but a precious echo of Our Father in Heaven who is insistently inviting our lowly soul to attend to His consoling voice. *"Be still and know that I am God"*. Yes He is Our Father in heaven. As St. Augustine instructs, it is true that the wings of heaven graciously extend to all his creation in such manner that he is closer to us than we are to ourselves.

Therefore, I take the opportunity of these few lines to gladly endorse and propose the publication of this rich volume to memoirs of the author to the vast number of its fortunate readers as part of her encouragement to the faith by sharing her unique and personal encounters with the divine.

May God richly bless the author and readers of these unique expositions! Amen.

Bishop Hyacinth O. Egbebo, MSP.

✑ PROLOGUE ✑

Many of us journey through life with a realisation that there is
more to us than the physical. We are present to the existence
of a soul different in nature to what our five senses perceive.
Often we experience in our souls a longing that cannot be
satisfied with the mundane activities of our everyday life. Deep
in our spirits, we understand that the soul yearns for something
beyond this realm, for connection to its source, for union with
the divine. We seek the face of God. As Saint Augustine
said, "our hearts are restless until they rest in God". Even
with this realisation, some of us find it difficult to experience
the connection with the divine that our souls yearn for.

In these pages Rev Sr Freda shares her personal journey
toward the divine – the ups and downs, the doubts, fears,
reassurances, glimpses of love and light. In challenging times
I often remember an experience she shared with me over a
decade ago. One of the times in her life when she went through
immense difficulty, she was moved to give up on a course of
action she had embarked on in the service of God. While
waiting to communicate her decision, she had a vision. She
saw herself standing in front of a large and intense wall of
fire. She saw Jesus standing on the other side of the fire and
desired to go to him. She braised herself and passed through
the fire to the other side. Jesus asked her "how did you feel
when you passed through that fire?" Her obvious response
was "uncomfortable, pained, hot". Jesus replied, "but if you
hadn't passed through that fire, you wouldn't be close to me
now". At the point, she woke up and understood that the
challenge she was facing was meant to make her stronger,

strengthen her faith, and bring her closer to Christ. She was encouraged and decided to maintain her commitment.

Sr Freda has dedicated her life to the service of the poor in the congregation of the Religious Sisters of Charity. She empowers young people and women through counselling, workshops, and seminars on various subjects including health, marriage, child protection, and spirituality. She also empowers the poor and cares for the elderly in her community through sustenance and community development projects. In addition, she teaches in seminaries and various parishes.

She has been an inspiration to me watching her go through each day in total service. I have been privileged to share my journey with her, and vice versa. She has been a confidant, a pillar of strength and an amazing big sister to me.

It is my hope and prayer that this book inspires the reader and provides encouragement, support, and light.

- Juliet Ehimuan Chiazor

∽ INTRODUCTION ∽

In modern times there is a search for a deeper and more transcendent meaning of life at both personal and global levels. There is a hunger for intimacy and love that cuts across all facet and levels of society. There is a desire to connect with the core of life. These have led some people to search in places that are in most cases less productive and unsatisfying. People have adopted strange habits to curb their inner longing or ease their inner pain. Some people are not aware of what they are searching for. Others are aware of their inner longing and are looking for ways to satisfy this longing. These have led many people to take solace in working all the time to avoid encountering their loneliness. The result of this is sadness, anger and stress which have led to all kinds of diseases. I believe that the longing in the human heart is for God.

Spirituality draws the whole of me into relationship with God. Christian Spirituality has to do with having a love relationship with God and a desire to deepen that relationship and live it out in everyday life. We are born from love, and surrounded by love (*Gaudium Epes*). Love is our core and essence and the point of connection with the Divine. The word was made flesh and lived among us. In our day to day experience we develop a relationship with this word that is made flesh (Jn. 1:14). Jesus is the word of God; in him we are shown how to be fully alive and authentically human in relationship with God. Therefore our Christian journey moves us towards finding the meaning of life in Christ. The Christian journey leads us to the path of maturing in love and intimacy. This brings us to a level where charity becomes essential as we move towards love of self and neighbour. Paramount therefore to the love of God is the love of self and the love of neighbour. This requires self development, growth and self sacrifice. It requires dying to the false self so that the true self can grow. Unless a grain of wheat falls to the ground and dies it remains a single grain, but if it dies it yield a rich harvest (Jn.12-24). The true self has enormous potential to reveal the image of love that we are which sometimes is hidden or lost as a result of self preservation. 'For anyone who wants to save his life will lose it; but anyone who loses his life for my sake will find it' (Mt. 16-25).

I believe that the way to find our true self is to become present to God's love in all things. To feel love in the breeze that wheezes across our faces; in the drumming of our heart beat; in the singing of the birds; in the cotton of dew upon the grass; in everything small and big. To become aware that we are created in love; surrounded by love, infused in love; filled with love and called to love. How can we long for love when we are surrounded by so much love? How can we be stressed up and afraid when we are cherished, cradled, cuddled, sheltered and protected by Divine love? We must tune to the Divine current so that love may become real in our lives. The journey of life moves us into the transformative awareness of God's presence in the world and in our life. We become conscious of the Divine reality within. As John of the Cross puts it in his poem (*The living flame*), "How gently and lovingly you (God) awakes in my bosom, where you (God) dwells secretly and alone! In your sweet breathing, full of blessing and glory, how delicately you (God) inspire my love."[1] The journey of life is a love relationship; an invitation towards intimacy with God.

---

[1] St John of the Cross, *The Collected Works of St. John of the Cross*, trans. By Kieran Kavanaugh, and Otilio Rodriguez (Washington, DC: Institute of Carmelite Studies, 1973).

The word intimacy when described in etymological term comes from two Latin words *intimus* and *intimare* meaning innermost, to hint at, announce, publish and make known.[2] Therefore the journey of life involves going within to encounter our true self and get rid of all sorts of falsehood and come to a tangible sense of a divine presence within. The journey of life is a sacred movement of love among us. God's Love is always with us. What we need is to be present to that love in prayer, in silence, in work and in everything. Intimacy with God restores our soul to God's likeness (Eph. 4:22-24; Col. 3:9-10). When we develop a personal relationship with God, we become open to the Holy Spirit that is, the God that dwells within, then like St. Augustine we can say, "God is closer to me than myself"[3]. We come to a place of intuitive awareness where we are guided by grace. This leads to emptiness and complete surrender. It also lead us to a sacred space were everything that symbolises or images God becomes a source of intimacy with God. We become aware of the presence of Love in all things; therefore the presence of God in all things. To be tickled by the song of birds and insects, to inhale the fragrance of flowers and the seasons. This is the foundation of the experience of Divine intimacy. This is allowing God's love to embrace us in everything. This sort of intimate encounter with God frees the heart from fear. We encounter our mysterious depth. This is what it means to be truly alive and Christian.

Jesus said, "I have come that they might have life and have it to the full (Jh.10:10)". It is the will of Jesus that we have a relationship with the Divine that fills us with abundant life and lightens our burden. This book is compiled from my journal, my experiences and journey towards a love relationship with the divine that

---

[2]   A. M. MacDonald, Ed. Chambers Etymological English Dictionary 1964
[3]   Augustine, Confessions. Edited and trans. By John K. Ryan (New York: Image book/Doubleday 1960).

has transformed my life and brought me to where I am today. Hopefully it will help the reader to get in touch with their own experiences of God and the reality of God relating lovingly in our world today. For others this book will awaken in them a desire for intimacy with God or a hope that this is possible and that their longing and hunger for God can truly be satisfied.

PONDERING

I walked silently through the garden. A stream flowed nearby. The sun had found the dancing water between the trees. I raised my eyes to stare over the glitter where the walls of the house rose and the vast coloured sprawl of the large palm trees brocaded the stream as it splash against the small rock. The birds were singing and the cricket called out to each other for attention. I could hear the gentle breeze whistling through the palms. The sun bright and hot burns through my neck:

As I walked through the garden
My heart began a prayer
God is present here I ponder
As true as in the Eucharist

Then my heart began to thunder
Talk to me! Talk to me!! Talk to me!!!
Talk to me, I know you are nearer
Today we celebrate together
Tomorrow, passion's pearl we gather

I can hear your voice sounding nearer
I want your attention solely dearer
I feel you close warmly tender
I need love's passion lingering stronger

I walked through the garden
My heart raised in praises
Then in the midst of birds singing
A bird called out in phrases
God has called, heart leapt in praises
To this God that lift's my burden

REFLECTION

Sometimes we feel burdened and empty and very much alone. We look for the company of people to fill our emptiness. Other times we compensate by eating too much, drinking too much, or watching too much television. We try to fill our emptiness and loneliness in many different ways. Sometimes our body is in the present while our mind is either in the past or in the future. We can be segmented and dissatisfied. The truth is nothing can satisfy us or fill us except the Lord Jesus. St. Augustine must have experienced this when he exclaimed, "I am made for you oh God and my soul is restless until it rest in thee". No matter what we have, either material wealth or intelligence we will not be content until we place our heart in God who is our source.

We encounter God only by becoming present to ourselves and to our environment. In this presence we become aware of God who satisfies our inner longing. How can we be present to ourselves? We can be present to ourselves by becoming aware of our breathing because, the mind tends to stray to the past or the future while the body is mostly in the present. When we become aware of our breathing we bring the mind into the present. Now how do we become aware of our breathing? We pay attention to the air as it pass through our nostrils into our bodies and to feel the warm air as it comes out of our bodies through our nostril. In focussing and paying attention to our breathing, we bring our mind and body into a union of presence. We become aware of the present moment. We stand a better chance of meeting the God who declared to Moses, 'I Am That I Am'; not I was and not I will be, but I am; the omnipresent God. We also stand a better chance of becoming aware of the fact that, there is more to life than we can see.

STRUGGLING

I stood by the edge of a stream. My heart lurched in my chest as the stream left its water-course: winding round the palm tree towards the back of the beautiful house. I walked from the garden searching and seeking within. Wondering what I must do. I picked up my pen and paper, my mind became alive. I felt free to move around the pages. I began to write, my reflection, meditation and insights came alive on paper. Words began to dance before my eyes my pen seems to have taken on a life of its own. Every search, every struggle began to take shape on the paper.

Struggling with love, struggling with life
Struggling to die, death to life
Within the depth, a call to self
Still struggling with love, struggling with self

The force of love tickles with fear
The root of fear sprouts to dare
What I fear, I can't understand
Yet struggling with love, struggling with life

Lost is the heart that girder in fear
Love is the prompt that brings to life
This struggle must cease, chortle to death
Life must be lived, lived in love.

Must struggle to love, must struggle to live
Exhausted words crumbled in tears
Stretched to their limit, they shear.

As if exhausted the words stopped dancing, it has reached its limit. I no longer have words, but I felt a strange struggle. A voice within gentle prompts me not to be afraid.

REFLECTION

Sometimes we feel a strange struggle within us. We wonder if others feel the same way. Something within, draws us to a different space. We are lured and seduced yet we are afraid to take the necessary step. This maybe because we are not sure of what is happening to us or because we are afraid to leapt into the unknown. A voice within gently prompts us not to be afraid. Yet we want to hold on to what is familiar; what we are comfortable with; the image we project to the world; the mask we are familiar with that hides our insecurity. Yet we are invited to love ourselves and be free. It is by being intimate with the self that I begin to discover the God within. I become aware that I am the image of God therefore the image of love. And like St. Augustine I become aware that we are made for love.

To be truly alive we must be open to constant change and renewal, so that life does not pass us by and we do not become stagnant. In prayer and contemplation God gives us the grace to take risk and to journey into our innermost self and encounter our true self, this is the foundation of self intimacy. As we become more intimate with self, we are filled with joy and gratitude to God who created us.

LONELINESS

Life is ticking away lured steadily to its end
Heart beats in counsel you have not really lived
You are dumb to the music of life
Stiff you fail to dance to the music of life

Gentle breeze tickled my ears, to mend one must love
God is in the living, have you lived your life?
Lots of feelings danced past like breeze in a field
You long for the new as darkness enfold your soul

Like a sharp grass loneliness cuts through the heart
The search within as quiet as the night
Creator's love ripples through the earth
Yet this experience a shadow unfelt

I thought and prayed with hope in sight
Love might pass this way someday
Or someone a hand of care extend
Giving love in endless measure
Joy within burst to sight
The feeling of love a sound repose

SEARCHING

Where is God found, I often wonder; in the heart of people or in creation? I am beginning to see things differently. God's secret place is in the garden and this garden is within us and around us. It is the heart and core of everything. We can only see it through the eyes of the heart. Sometime ago as I walked through the garden I took shelter under some palm trees bowing down over a stream. I watch the water flowing; intimately splashing against the rocks boosting out in splashes like the sparkle of light. I felt surrounded by life and beauty. I have being searching for an insight into the depth of life. I have read the Bible from cover to cover and attended as many societal prayers as I can manage. Yet I continue to search; what is life about?

I know within me that there is more to life than our visible experiences. I have search for a long time for the core of life; for the truth to burst out from within the midst of life. I believe that there is more to life; there is a depth that is beyond our struggles. My soul is searching longing for answers.

I search; search and I search
I know not what I seek
The pull is acute and bleak
Yet I know not what I seek

There is more in life than toil
There is more than victuals and foil
The more seems arduous to clutch
Yet imminent; so close I nudge

The struggle in me the more must notch
The grief in me the more must touch
The darkness in me the more must light
Lest cease to live, just exist I slide

The moon and sun something must light
The cloud and sky something must hide
The truth is near, close to the more
The light of truth beckons me closer
Reveals the more to hide no more

PONDERING

There is a longing in my heart. A pull to something I cannot understand. This longing has been in me over a period of time. There is a restlessness within that seeks for calm. In prayer I cry and stretch for something hard to understand. I am torn between the sky and the land; between freedom and bondage. I feel called to make a choice between light and darkness, good and evil, love and indifference. How can I describe what I feel? How can I describe my experience? There is more behind the visible, a depth that lures me. There is a pain within that frightens me, something beyond my control. Sometimes I desire to connect, other times the pain is too much I withdraw. In this ambiguity of feelings the restlessness continued.

There must be more to our lives. There must be a mission for the human person on earth. Something is luring me to a depth I cannot understand. I began to feel that there is more to life than we can see. There is a depth that only those with single minded focus can glimpse. We have to struggle to become aware of the depth of our being. There is something hidden that nudges our souls.

I pondered for weeks within and without
What am I about, thought I know, really I don't
Within, a still silence that hits like the night
Without, chaotic like the roaring of the sea

What is life about I wondered in fright
Thought I know, but sorry I don't
Creation speaks a language hard to heed
Seems I'm deaf to within and without
What is life's meaning pondered I day and night
I cease to search, content just to be
Suddenly out of living came an answer to me
God is present, as moment by moment I live

God is found in the present always within and without
My choice is clear as moment by moment I live
In you a fragment of me, in me a fragment of you
God is in the present, in you in all, and in me.

REFLECTION

Have you ever felt that there is more in life than you can see or imagine? That there is a bigger picture that eludes your vision? That the primary concern of God is simpler and gentler than what you can comprehend? You get the feeling that the world is vast and you are like a drop in the ocean in this wilderness of space? Something in you desire to connect with this depth. You find yourself searching and seeking in all sorts of places.

When we focus too much on the concerns of this world and our daily struggles we will become distracted and out of touch with the depth of life. Our daily activities, though important are a very tiny part of who we are and what we are about. Yet something tells us that we are unique and special. We get the feeling that someone beyond ourselves is close to us and is working for us, inviting us to expand and experience ourselves in full.

When we spend some time in the day to get in touch with our feelings and thoughts we come to the present moment then we begin to experience the depth of life. Let us pray together for a moment. Become aware of your breathing as you breathe in and out; of your heartbeat and your pulse if it helps put your hand against your chest. This action of becoming aware of your breathing will bring you to the present moment. You will gradually become tuned to the rhythm of your being as it harmonises with creation. You will then begin to feel the love that ripples through creation.

FIRE OF LOVE

In the silence of prayer, I became convinced that I am created for a purpose. My presence in this world is not an accident. This realisation changed my attitude and perception of the world. Each of us reflects an aspect of God. We are call to live out the spark of God in our world. We are different, but together we tell one story. Together we make deeper and more meaningful sense. We are connected to everything else. Why do we live as if we have no source; no base or no foundation?

It seem to me that people have changed creation's trail
That people were meant to move
differently in ways still unknown
There is a glimpse from God of where we are meant to trail
Oh! But see the way we have gone
From burning flame that warms the
earth to ice that freeze it dead
What is wrong with loving another, why
these fears that make us groan?

Life a risk is meant to be lived in joy, sorrow or tears
Whatever our choice, the risk is great love still abounds
For lost of love is lost of God, where can God be found
Pain of love my potion for joy, love within ignites

This fire of love burns within, God ignites within
This love within share with all, else God is hidden within
This fire of love must burn, its time the heart comply
This fire of love must burn that all may feel its warmth.

REFLECTION

There is a stage in life when we become dissatisfied with material wealth and long for something deeper and more lasting; when love and relationships become more important than success and achievements. We fall in love with something or someone we cannot comprehend. There is a hunger for love that burns within because, we are made in love and made for love. At this point in our life, our soul begins to yearn for its source and essence which is love. Some of us search for love in the wrong places; in unhealthy relationships, in material wealth, in power and in possession. We are looking for quick love full of unhealthy desire and short term excitement. The truth is, this love is false and brings with it loneliness and sorrow.

True love takes time and presence; a reflective awareness that brings us to the depth of things. It starts with simple prayers and devotion to meditation on the word of God in the bible and to contemplation. If we stay with true love or a desire for true love with its pain and sweetness, we begin to experience a personal passionate connection with the Divine. From then on, every experience; every love relationships and every encounter flows from this passionate connection with the Divine. We get to a space where we are no longer empty but full of happiness from within and no longer crushed by pains and sorrows of this world.

BATTLE WITHIN

Something within seems to be burbling up, seeking to burst out like the gush of water from a broken tap. There is a strangeness surrounding me. There is a battle within me. Six months later 1 wrote in my journal:

Trembling like a leaf, my fears are true
Oh God; 1 am sliding too fast below
Sliding as darkness enfold my soul
No safe haven to anchor my soul
I am gliding too fast below.

Heart throbbing as swiftly as can be
A bittersweet tension as painful as can be
A crave that lures, yet hurls away
A fear so daring, yet endearing it sways
An urge to flee, yet to cleave and survey

I am the image of a two-levelled dance
Why this lure to be and not to be
I am torn in two, puissant and fragile
Just a chum of a naked heart
Forcing forth fear that lures to flee

But from whom, only from self
The self a reality hard to conceal
Running away a birth of conceit
It is good to care sometime someday
Painful as it may be, why not today.

REFLECTION

The Lord loves us with an endless love and God wants us to love him, for we are precious in his sight. Let us be confident, then, to turn to the Lord to open the gate of our heart, to know his living presence, and our fears will disappear like the morning mist upon the earth. Cast your burden unto the Lord for the Lord hears and answers. Say to God, I am scared of so many things, of the way people can hurt me badly; of the way they treat me with contempt and disrespect, and what they can say about me; I am scared of crimes of sickness, unexplainable pains and unexpected reactions towards me.

Say to God, I am scared of my reactions to people and things; of my weaknesses and sinfulness. I feel so insecure. There are so many challenges in my day that overwhelm me. Lord I know you love me and I feel your presence close to me and I am important to you. In this wilderness of confusion and uncertainties, help me to trust in you and remain focused on you. I love you Lord and my heart yearns for you please dear Lord help me to face the future with trust in your loving care, so that no matter what happens, I will always trust in you and remain in your love.

CONNECTION

It is sometimes so difficult to care. Yet when we care it is impossible not to be affected by people's experiences. Their pains touch our heart and help us to look at ourselves critically and examine how we live our own lives. It helps us to put things in perspective and to know what is important. When we empathise with people, we feel what they feel in the depth of our being. This brings us to a deeper understanding of the other person and the self. It connects us to the others person in an intimate loving manner. The fact is, when we empathise with people we are filled with compassion and understanding this makes us less judgemental. It is not easy and takes years of loving; but if we know who we are, we will know that the potential is within us lying dormant.

This realisation that we are connected and affect each other, came to me as l walked in a garden, everything have a natural order. Life and death comes and goes, but each in its proper time. God's will is always available to us; we can open up to it or close up. Our choice determines whether we live joyfully or sorrowfully on earth. It is important to encourage positive thinking; to surround ourselves with issues of love and compassion. God is in all things and all people; no one can change that even for a second.

In the middle of the garden I see
The ground a carpet of green
Closely drawn to a tree
A friendship began with thee.

In silence the tree propose
Draw nearer or flee
Spell bound I'm drawn by the tree
Closer than I care to be.

I stood one with the tree
Speaking in silence to me
The leaves sprawling and free
Danced to the tune of the breeze

Spiral and straight branches
Twist to chart a deal
Leave tired to be
Getting old they coil

Dry leaves began to fall
Close to the root of the tree
Dead leaves sucked into the soil
To nourish and feed the tree

Silently the tree intone
Green for food; colour for beauty
A job for all; a reason and duty
If life must stay with thee

This is creation real and true
We are fashioned each for a reason
Why fear to die; death begins another
That the world might live its due
The dead is within the earth
Nourishing and giving it life

When your work on earth is done
To die really is order
Death a birth into another
That our work may still be done
In the silence of the tree
Death a treat no more to be

REFLECTION

Sometimes we are so afraid of death that we close up and refuse to love. We are afraid of getting hurt, of dying to self or of anything to do with death. The truth is we end up not living life to the full; protecting ourselves excessively; taking so many expensive preclusions yet at the appointed time we die anyway. Is it not better to live life in abundance and trust God? Who among us can extend our life for a second if it is not the will of God? If we realise this, death cease to be a treat. Then we can confidently say death where is your sting? When we develop an intimate relationship with God, then we know God cannot forget us. For the bible say, 'Does a woman forget her baby at the breast, even if these forget... I will never forget you'. The evil one keeps us locked in doubt so that we think we are all alone and must struggle with God to stay alive. Dear friends it is in God that 'we live and move and exist' Acts 17:28.

GOD SPEAK

Out I went to take a walk myself nature to give
The birds singing their song flying through the sky
Flowers open their beauty to greet the world around
Sky a giant blanket stretched to embrace with joy
Bees bussing around the flowers drawn by their beauty

Drawn by the beauty, the flowers words of warmth
The dry the blooming and those yet to bud
This is my life in creation nature seems to say
God is speaking here and now hearts filled with joy
Life a mixture of old and new and life yet to be

Came a prayer to my lips to the creator of us all
That we may see what is old and grasped what is new
We may hope for what is yet and grasped what is now
And Lord that we may see they all spring from you

At times of retreat contentment is sought
To find the divine in all around
To feel God's love ripples through creation
As around the garden I walked, peace I began to feel
In nature love surrounds, holding us close to the real.

REFLECTION

Sometimes we are so busy doing our own things. We are not even aware of the beauty of creation. Neither do we observe that God is communicating with us in every fragment of creation. If we stop even for a moment each day and become fully conscious of our surrounding, we will suddenly realise that we are surrounded by a force or current moving us all the time. We are protected, preserved, privileged, sheltered, shielded and therefore secure.

BROKEN HEART

Sometimes painful things happen in our lives, we are called to experience suffering cause by people around. We begin to question, how can God allow so much pain? Yet we know that even Jesus suffered pain. In my pain, 1 saw the people shouting in anger, determined to crucify Jesus. The world rejects what it cannot understand. Jesus does not fit into the order of things. I saw people hurting, betraying, persecuting and inflicting pain on each another. Then in prayer I looked through the eyes of Jesus; I saw compassion, peace and forgiveness for people's ignorance. I saw hope that someday these people might come to know the truth and the truth shall set them free. I looked through the eyes of Jesus; all I could see is love and forgiveness. Therefore I bear my pain in silence and love, forgiving all wrong done to me, so that my eyes may become like the eyes of Jesus; to see only what Jesus sees and to look only where Jesus looks.

Dreaded pain, sorrow, loneliness all in tears
A heart burning, aching accused with fear
Self willed, no fear, all complaints will end
Evil spoken of what's not like brute beast send

By trickery they amuse, unsightly blots on souls
They seduce to sin, their prey the most stable of souls
Armed with bows and spears, cruelly they pierce
Cursed with destruction, they shatter the earth
Their weapons are words, and fear of folks
Oh it's suffering snivelling in and out

Save us God, least we are crushed
Bring order to chaos and save the crushed
Liberate your people that they come to glow
Troubled I pray forsake not your own
Ah! It's suffering everywhere purifying all to glow

SUFFERING

Created to be God-like, gentle in all that is call
In delight self is given to work; to all
Happy, willing devoted gave self gave all
A fighter, bound to win, confident, never to fall

Eyes deep, tears roll like a broken tap
Drained, saddened, forsaken by all
Truth turned around to hurt, body sapped
Out of lies pain emerges drifting off it saps
Dreams gone like the night, life deems a pall

Soul into darkness lures to the haze solitude
The world squalls to a blanket of bugs
Creature a muddle of reed, subtle and rude
The world contract like stream in a mug

Heart pricked like a dance in the rose garden
Heart beats like rambling in the heavens
A deep loneliness, like the silence of graves
Deadness, like the fall of dry leaves
Drifting in pain like air through the leaves

Falling deep into emptiness into the depth of void
In the grip of silence light battles to life
Struggling for a grip light shuttles to sight
Help from without to aid this fight
Only the Divine can bring to might
Stilting in glum I remain in darkness

REFLECTION

Suffering does not always come from our external experiences. Sometimes it comes from an inner longing; a thirst for something more. Sometimes we feel that we have lost contact with something or someone beyond ourselves. Our prayer becomes dry and we begin to question, 'why did God call us'. We remember our past intimacy with God and our sins become visible to us. Everything seems to be wrong and we are so broken and divided. Our weaknesses hunt us and they stick to us like a shadow. We fall on our knees in tears to God, our heart aches and we are unable to find consolation anywhere. Our pain is compounded by people's misunderstanding. We have two options; we can either wait on the Lord trustingly or we can look for consolation in worldly things. Whatever choice we make helps us to live from our depth or in falsity.

DARKNESS

I long for God; I thirst for God. I feel unworthy, inadequate and my sins are always before me; what a terrible state. Within the light of God the darkness and shadows around me have become more visible. Even though I am confident of God's love, I am afraid that I have lost contact. My prayer is dry my weaknesses are always before me. Sometimes I wonder why God called me. God knows my weaknesses why did God call me? Oh! I remember the past intimacy I shared with God. Why are my weaknesses hunting me persistently? God is so faithful and I am so faithless. Save me Lord I surrender to you.

I tried to hide away from God. I no longer know my own mind. I asked the Lord to help me discover my thoughts. Who am I? What am I really about? Sometimes I wonder what force is drawing me. I feel such a sinner yet so cared for. I shouted, 'I love you so much God' and fell on my knees and began to cry. My sins struck me like a whip and pain shook my body to the very core of my being.

The heavens unfastened revealing the fullness of the sun
Its ray thrown over the landscape in sprays of fire
Then into hiding went the sun like a fearful child
The stars began to peep through the sheet of cloud.

Awaken in my soul a little voice surged to light
Mend your ways free your heart let go in love
Hold with love the weak and strong within
Darkness can see whispers the night
You are like a feast with no entrance in.

Fares eyes stared at me move before you drift
This is the river of life alone you must glide
I stared hard conjuring a bridge from death to life
The strong must die that the weak may come to birth
Down the deep I went gasping for air
Sucked into the deep like an insect into a spider's web

I faced up to the fading side of me
Grieved to know a path never walked aright
God help! Shadows are surging mightily to sight
So much to learn in this darkness of soul

Courage a tool aid the leap into the night
In entering, hidden growth sprang to sight
Only in faith can one leap and become truly whole
Afraid to retreat, frightened to continue what a plight

Pain cuts through the heart like moon through the night
Yet it's time to face the self, time to go within
Tired of being false begged to be true
Tired of goodness a ritual, grateful to be true
Stunned in silence the end is yet in sight.

REFLECTION

In other for growth to happen, we need to encounter our true self. This involve going into the void of our being and getting to know what is true within and what is false. It requires honesty and a sincere desire to be intimate with the true self. The true self is the individual's inborn potential for a unique personality, the source of authenticity and spontaneity.[4] Encounter with our deepest self creates so much pain because we need to shed what is false so that what is true can glow. Jesus puts it well when he said: "Unless a grain of wheat falls to the ground and dies it yields a single grain but when it dies it yields a rich harvest" Jh. 12:24.

---

[4] D.W. Winnicott, The Maturational Process and the Facilitating Environment (New York: International Universities Press, 1960) 141-142

FORGIVENESS

I asked forgiveness for my sins. When I considered God's wonders
I trembled with fear. I prayed for mercy as I saw my sins before me.
Then I experienced a disturbing forceful contact with something
hard to describe. It was so separate, so great and so powerful. It
was a magnetic peaceful feeling yet a dreadful fearful experience.
I had an awesome fear, a fascination and a burning desire to hold
on yet to leave everything and follow.

The day is lonely and the earth is dark
The sting of enemies stronger than bees
The claws of sin festers my wounds
I fret in rage for what has been.

Time is going the days are short
Their words a knife cut through my heart
No help forthcoming no hope in sight.

Then a voice began a speech
All is good that harbours the storm
Eyes on God a joy to souls
The word of God a haven of peace

Then the eyes of my heart clearer in sight
The secret of my heart wisdom to teach
The bones in my body danced with thrill
The depth of my heart a tear to God
The haven of peace I dwell again.

REFLECTION

Have you ever found yourself in prison and everybody is welding more bars on the gate so that you cannot get out? You looked around and found that you are the one giving them the bars to close you in. This is a terrible feeling and this is what happens when we allow people to control our lives. Sometimes they do more than control our lives they become the critical voices that keep telling us that we cannot move further; that our sins are too much and we cannot move closer to God. If we listen to them we will give up hope and lost contact with the God who loves us so much. I was once like this, until in prayer God taught me how to be authentically me. It does not matter what people think. If your conscience is clear that you are doing what God wants and you are not unjust to anyone else then by all means keep doing what you are doing. Sometimes the fear of rejection or criticism prevents us from doing the good we would like to do. Therefore many good deeds end in our mind but are never carried out. If you surrender to God, you will be filled with courage and God will help you to gradually see yourself the way God sees you.

RIVER OF LIFE

In prayer I came before a sheet of cloud
Patently I waited for the cloud to lift
I felt something luring my heart to love
Something is touching the depth my being
Someone is tickling my heart to move
Then I felt lifted by the cloud
I was moving yet remained still
I felt full, loved and fondled into life

I came to a river of cloud
The voice in my heart lured me to cross
As I crossed I felt sucked into the midst
The voice said, remove the yoke you are carrying
I became aware of two yokes on my back
Let them go and you can cross

I tried to let them, but only one was dropped
Like a magnet the other was attached to my body
The voice said, one yoke is your refusal to accept yourself
The other your refusal to let go of people's opinions
My heart began to beat erratically
Yet the river of life lures me to cross

The voice said, I cannot carry you across
You must cross on your own
One day you would understand
Beside the river of cloud love beckons me
I let go and surrendered to the unknown
Waiting patiently, love must find a way.

Christians are called to reflect the loving face of Christ to the world. People must see in us what they cannot find elsewhere in the world. It is not enough to say we belong to Christ, we must proclaim that Christ lives in us. My heart is so hurt and full of pain. Can I ever say I have become Christ? Yet today I am reminded to love with the heart of Christ. When pain and anxiety prevent me from being Christ I pray, 'Help me Lord to love with the heart of Christ'. Let love be the lens for which we view people and experiences. Let love be the foundation, from which all our thoughts reflections and actions flow. Then each of us can say personally, 'it is not I Christ lives in me'.

Restless flesh a time to rest
You beat God's tune night and day
Pump life's blood though the chest
Air a friend the potion you caress

Restless flesh a time to rest
Within your depth love is felt
In you sorrow and pain lie to rest
Happiness and joy from you is felt

Restless flesh a time to rest
Your work of vision rest today
Be still and see his peace display
Wait for the maker you seek today

Restless flesh it's time to rest
Lie fallow and shelter to rest
Heal the wound the joy display
Then fruit in plenty you sure would bear.

REFLECTION

Sometimes we have a strong desire to be good and holy. To follow Jesus in a single minded way. Our sins and pains get in the way of our good intention. We begin to feel that we are not good enough for God then we give up and refuse to answer to the divine invitation. We must know that, nothing can separate us from God. In spite of our sins the invitation to be close to God remains. We must move towards our good intention and God will meet us where we are and will gently draw us towards our good desires.

I put on a mask that is acceptable to the society. Something is luring me out of the mask. It is frightening yet I want to be real. I sat to pray and my life was mirrored to me. I saw my falsehood, my weaknesses, and my lack of commitment. I could see my unworthiness how can God love me? How can I claim to love God? Who am I trying to impress? A voice whispered into my heart, God loves the real you open up and bloom. I felt vulnerable and afraid.

Silence deep dark silence within and without
In the silence lots were spoken clear and true
Heart a film, my soul its actress acting my life's replay
Clearly I see the falsehood hidden within the self.

The first heat of denial finally did subside
This is truth the real me long hidden away
The ground lost it form rowing me like a boat
Its mouth opens wide, to swallow me to its darkness.

To stay no longer safe, to jump the more dangerous
Just plunge off the land into the deep I fell
Fear, I would be swallowed snapped out of life
Come with me, but no, I must go alone

Darkness, loneliness, confusion, piled deep within
Love to be good, not to be good, life is lived in love
Afraid of fear, fear is good this is where to be
So to grow, one must die policy the earth display
Grain must die so to grow that lot of wheat it yields
Die I must, so to live policy the earth display

Darkness and light side by side live within as friends
There is growth within, but darkness still at play
Knowing a pain, yet love must bring the self to birth
Deeper I go into the self, trembling what else is there.

REFLECTION

Sometimes we place emphasis on projecting an acceptable image. We focus on hiding any unacceptable behaviours or attitude within. We put so much energy in trying to keep this image going. This is sad because when we become intimate with our true self and let our mask drop we encounter God in whose image we are created. We discover love our essence; eminence; reason and status. We discover our potential, own our strength, hold our weakness and know that God loves us no matter what.

GOD'S FAITHFULNESS

A full moon lit the garden. The brightness reflected to overshadow the dark night. The garden was big and shaded by trees and flowers. The night was peaceful. I could hear the birds singing and the crowing of the frogs as creation merged in harmonious symphony. The house was situated deep into the garden and hidden by trees. Grateful for the cool night after a very hot day, I stretched my hands in front of me and closed my eyes. I filled my lungs with cool air; sat on a stone perched between the hedges and leaned back against a tree. I stirred at the stars and felt at one with creation. Yet the darkness within threatened to overpower me.

My heart extends eyes emerge
The core an eye a sight to see
Across the sea a figure emerged
The yell from me, a fright of heart

A hand unfurl come to me
It can't be me, my core erupt
The gale a fright that chilled my soul
The figure a pull beyond my strength

Onto the void as stiff as can be
The figure a lure beyond my strength
Gently I'm lured my focus on you
The closer I come; the further from you

Depart from me less I perish
Hands unfurl, held me steady
Trust and faith the clue to be steady
Learn to walk you must on water
Hence in the void you'll fail to stand

REFLECTION

Sometimes we feel a strong pain within. We seem not to be sure of where our life is going. We become aware of our sinfulness and limitation. Some of us struggle with ourselves trusting in God's mercy and power to save. Others just give up and stop trying. Despite our fears, we must plunge into this darkness trusting in the Divine Light. We must go within our being to find out who we are. We must trust that God will not let us down. In psalm 23 the psalmist declared, 'though I walk through the valley of shadow of death I shall fear no evil' for God is with me to comfort me.

HAVEN OF PEACE

In prayer I remained silent before the Lord. I saw Jesus washing the apostle's feet and watched their resistance, confusion and shock. Jesus turned to me and invited me into the circle. I felt surrounded by love. He looked right into my eyes, I felt a warmth go through my body. He began to wash my feet so gently, delicately as if holding a pearl. It felt very good. I was so overwhelmed with love I began to cry. The tears just kept flowing like a broken tap. I allowed myself to be surrounded by God's forgiveness. I felt able to forgive all wrongs done to me. I remained silent before the Lord. In this silence of God's Love, I became comfortable with myself. I am now open to accept and love everyone else. I am not as judgmental or as scrupulous as I use to be. Yes the world has become a haven of peace.

∽ OCTOBER 1999 ∽

LIFE FROM DEATH

Today I prayed for peace and quiet. God is calling me to a deeper understanding of His perfect love. In all my experiences, God is continuously drawing me to a deep unconditional love.

Weak heart beats erotically
Unprepared the seed sprang
Counting, their business mind
World unprepared, changes they find

What is this, seed must die
A life to give, lives to save
To come to birth, seed must die
Depth of growth springs from death

What is this love that slay
Perfect radical love that saves

REFLECTION

When we look at the world very carefully and we reflect on how things grow. We will notice that for every growth there must be a death. If you plant a seed, in order for the seed to grow, it must die. A plant flowers in order to have seeds, then the flower dies and the seed begins to form. I have come to realise that for me to grow some things have to die. I have to let go for my true self to bloom. God's invitation always has, 'come as you are'. In the depth of God's love you will be transformed.

ACCEPTANCE

Where is God found I wondered, in the heart of people; in creation? I really believe that the secret place of God can be found in the garden of our core. Sometime ago a woman lost her only son. What kind of faith prompted her to remain sane? A lot of people attended her son's burial. They all cried with the woman. It was a great surprise that she lost her only son. Without any husband or any other child her sorrow has just begun. While others were going away, I stood with the woman at the grave. I said to her, how did this happen? She replied, 'my son's death is strange. He saw a snake going towards a child. He ran after the snake and through a stone at it. As the snake turned, he grabbed it and threw it into the bush, in the process the snake bit his hand. He carried the child into the house and collapsed. He died in the hospital latter that day.' I am grateful she said, because my son's life was worthwhile. The son was fourteen years old. I left the woman feeling very grateful and yet sad.

Listening is not just about hearing what a person is saying but understanding the content and feelings in what they have shared. There are many truths and I must listen to people so that I can hear their truth, because in their truth they find God. The mother of the dead son shared with me her truth in that truth she found peace. Who am I, what is my truth?

THE LIGHT

I sat in the garden listening to the birds singing, the frogs crowing and the gentle breeze whistling through the palms. I felt an inner stillness and the earth seems to come to a hush. I closed my eyes and surrendered to the stillness. From within, I saw a dot of light, it became brighter and brighter until the whole of my body was filled with light. The light flowed out from within to form a spiral around my outer body, flowing from inside out and back again. The light danced around my body, displaying lots of colours that blend together in harmony. I felt my heart filled with love my skin tingled with warmth. I remain silent and felt cherished.

My story is strange but must be told
All must hear and wonder with me
I sat in the garden trying to pray
I close my eyes with a tune in my heart
A journey began that I have to share

A dot of light from heart expand
Drew me closer to the depth of heart
Deep in my heart the beat of drums
A veil conceal like cloud in the sky
Encircled with light like a spiral of sun

Darkness and shadows in a well of light
My sins and flaws a film to me
My pretence and guilt mock me to tears
I fell on my knees and began to cry
Pain and guilt united as one

Surrounded by light darkness is naked
Then I realise the nothingness of life
Save me Lord I am wretched in sin
The light in radiance, sprawl to might
Warmed the coldness in my heart
I am loved wretched as I am

I began to dance to the tune from my heart
Fear in fright, no more power to have
Free, I am free happy to dance
The self in truth sprang to being
It came to me, I really can fly
I began to surge higher in love
The burden I bore was fashioned by me

REFLECTION

Sometimes we suffer from scruples. We worry about sin and its effect rather than surrendering to God in humility and repentance. We allow our sins to discourage us. God truly loves us and wants us to come back in repentance and total trust.

There are times when we sense that God is calling us to do something different; to move from where we are to a different place. It is so difficult because most of the time we are very comfortable were we are. Other times we are too afraid to do something different. The more we look at Mary, the more we feel the power of movement to do and go where it is hard to believe with human intelligence. There has to be a different kind of intelligence that moves us to this space. We get this from meditation, were we are constantly looking at Jesus and Mary so much so that we begin to experience what they experience and we begin to feel what they feel. I wonder if this was the connection Paul felt when he said, 'it is not I Christ lives in me'; and St. Augustine when he exclaimed, "God is closer to me than myself."

TRINITY

I have encountered the divine and I am inspired. Jesus wants me to pray more and to pay more attention to his mother. I am thine o Mary! Take me under thy protection and keep me safe from sin. Jesus is calling me to a single hearted worship of him. There are many things he is preparing me to do, but only if I focus on God and avoid all bitterness. There is God in all Creation. I must search for God in all things.

Trinity the Son agreed to send
Salvation to gain for all to mend
Work is done son is gone
Spirit remains work proceed

Trinity again sits to send
Who must go whose turn to tend?
Send me I screamed filled with pride.

My turn to make an impact I thought
See my life a mess it's turned
Love's sacrifice I'm yet to hug
See, I'm sent but what is done

It's time to change this life anew
Oh mother, love in me renew
Trinity calls today anew
Trembling I said, grace me to go

Knowingly Trinity stared at me
Ready you are to go anew
Your strength my dear is found in me
Your courage is nothing apart from me

Go! Be Christ to all you meet
Go! Be light to all the nations
Go! Bring love to all you meet
Go! I'll be in all you fashion

So Trinity has sent today again
It's me and you alive to gain
Justice and peace our map display
The Holy Spirit our light and guard
Christ is you and me in the world today

I sat to pray I do not know whether in reality or in meditation the wall before me opened like a door, some instinct urged me to enter and I walked into darkness. I remained in this darkness for a while wondering what is happening to me. As my eyes adjusted to the darkness, I saw a cross and Jesus hanging on the cross. It was the bloodiest sight I have ever seen. I fell on my knees in front of the cross and began to cry. The blood flowed all over my body as if I was having a shower of blood. As I knelt there crying I raised up my head as if by invitation. I was looking directly into the eyes of Jesus. I felt warmth filled my body my pulse beat so strongly and my heart expanded. Something in me sprang into action. I started pulling the hand of Jesus away from the cross. As I removed one hand, Jesus shook his head and said to me. 'Do not try to remove me from the cross, share the cross with me'. I was speechless filled with wonder. How could anyone want to remain on the cross? Then I looked into the eyes of Jesus his truth played before me like a film. I became aware of his passion, his pain and the torture on his body. Despite the horror and the pain of this physical torture, Jesus suffered a greater pain, the pain of the heart. The pain of seeing the people he came to save crucified him; the so call Religious authority betrayed and disappointed him. However Jesus had an awareness that made a difference. He knew that the devil had confused the people, that some of them believed and were convinced that they were doing what was right by getting rid of the man of falsity who claimed to be God; they tried to trap him; looked for proof that he was a sinner; He was abandoned by friends, called names, accused of acquiring power from the devil. Jesus knew the people had got it wrong, because they had not removed the plank from their eyes so that they can see clearly... The devil has closed their mind with unbelief and self righteousness. Do you see yourself in these descriptions? Have you ever had this experience before? What was your reaction? What did you do?

In my prayer, I heard Jesus say, 'Not my will but your will be done'; in my case I said Father remove the pain so that I will no longer be the object of discussion'. Jesus said my heart is ready'; and I said my heart is broken. Jesus said 'Father forgive them for they know not what they do'; and I said Father be their judge, see how they are hurting me. Now Jesus has changed my perception; I have become aware that I need to love all people even when they are hurting me. I need not repay one wrong with another, but pray for those who persecute me. Now I know to be Christian is to see with the eyes of Jesus, to feel with his heart compassion and love even for those who hurt and persecute me. Then with the voice of Jesus I can say, 'Father forgive them for they know not what they do'.

Then I realise what I must do. Love people to birth, and die to all that is loveless. I can feel the pain of self sacrifice; the pain of selfless love. In the midst of this bloody sight, I gradually realise: Ah! Love is the answer my heart has come home to rest.

Sometimes we feel useless as if we are not wanted. We feel alone and different. We can either become closer to God, or we can try to become someone else and buy into what we do not believe in. If we take the second route we will finally become lonely, artificial and at the end of the road, we become isolated and stagnant. If we allow our heart to love and be open; we will move from loneliness into solitude were we are still before God. The bible says,' be still and know that I am God'. At the end of the road we will become intimate with God. We will feel loved and cherished by God in spite of who we are and what we are going through. Then God gradually move us to a different place; a different space. We become whole and connected or at least we feel drawn towards these.

SELFLESS LOVE

In prayer I was taken to a forest. I went deeper into the forest following a path until I came to an open space. A voice spoke to my heart, 'pray for perseverance'. I wondered if my life could be any tougher than it already is. The voice replied, every tough time has been my will for you. Then the voice said, 'you will carry my word to places'. I felt protected shielded and cherished. I surrendered to this warmth and felt loved. I remained still for a long time surrounded by so much peace.

Walking in the garden, silence embraced my soul
I sat on a stone, starring at nothing
Time must move, I said to myself
Yet something within, kept me steady
Overwhelmed with pain, I began to cry
Yet something within, kept me steady

My mind began a life of its own
I was in a valley surrounded by green
Gripped by fear of what is unknown
I began to run up the mountain
Strange, it seems my path was marked

I followed the path ahead of me
It's time to move I said to myself
Yet something within kept me steady
I reached the top, the mountain extend
I heard a voice call my name
Welcome home it says to me

My heart expand deeply in love
My home is here fear dispelled
The voice began to speak to me
This is you at one with all
Off the mountain as light as can be
Feeling like a bird I began to fly
Help me Lord least I perish

I am with you, never to perish
This is home, you're made to fly
The voice was gone no longer to be heard
Then I realise how empty I am
Yet in love you hold me steady
With tears in my eyes my gratitude to you
For this love that fill me up

DEEPLY IN LOVE

I sat in front of a crucifix to pray. I gazed at the crucifix for a long time then had the urge to close my eyes. The image of the crucifix remained within. I felt an overwhelming love and freedom. As I gazed, my heart began to fly. I was in my room yet not confined by the walls. I found myself in a thick forest climbing a mountain. I was shouting wonderful! Wonderful!! I felt as if I was not myself, but was at one with everything around me. I remained on this mountain for a long time and was reluctant to come down. I felt full and lightheaded. I was overwhelmed with joy and peace. I felt in love with creation. I am at home. Every breath I take has an echo of love. Everywhere I look is infused with love. God is everywhere in everything. Love is.... God is....

ONLY SON

I found myself before a tree
Darkness everywhere as dark as night
It seemed to me depression in the air
Yet the tree as common as can be
I stood my ground, staring at the tree

Slowly the eyes through darkness can see
The tree two braches joined together
This tree called common allures me near
A horrid sight shocked me to tears

As love bleeds in labour to birth of heart
Please I thirst, his cry of distress
A hand that whirls faster than air
Gave to drink vinegar on a shaft
I stood my ground, stating at the tree

Time is leeched to the tree in sight
A woman stood by laden with tears
Crying heartily for her son's plight
Numb with pain at the lover's bed
My sadness acute this son will die
I watched the mother crying for her son
I stood my ground, staring at the tree

A man with a spear I beg to spare
Pierced his side surge blood and water
The son slump dead, slipped to the stars
I stood my ground, staring at the tree

The rain came down, the earth in sorrow
Son held tight in his mother's arms
Death and life merge as one
I stood my ground, staring at the tree

Why this death and void of pain
The mother in silence, a look that pierce
My words are dumb to hearts of love
It's all for you, my son had to die

Go to the world apprise my people
My son had to die, to inspire your love
He loves all people new hearts are born
I stood my ground, staring at the tree

It become clear their yes is for me
I fell on my knees and began to weep
Mother and son, love true and deep
Please dear mother, teach me to love.

Darkness everywhere battles for power
A dot of light from depth emerged
It seem to me depression in the air
Slowly the eyes through darkness can see
Trees as one allure me nearer
A horrid sight shocked me to tears.

The world is plagued, love it fears
Shunned giddily alone it snaps
Bleeding in labour to await a birth
Stretched on a tree, open to snare
Time condensed, leeched to the tree
Halt with time the earth awaits

A woman stood-by saddened to tears
Crying heartily for her son's plight
Numbed with pain at this lovers bed
Grief surged, drowned my soul to sight
Love like a dove stilts to sight
Numb to fight pulse to light
A battle of thoughts spiral to sight
Why this death this path of pain

My words are dumb to heart of love
The mother in silence a look that pierce
Love bleeds to death that life it yields
It become clear, their yes is for all
Mother and son merge in love
Heaven and earth spun in union
Life is renewed, sprout from love

Signal of the new, sprung to birth
Love wound bleeds life's soul to birth
The imprint of love stamped my soul
Love sits in laughter chortles in might
I fell to my knee and began to weep
Please dear mother, teach me to love.

INTIMATE CONNECTION

I was silent before the Lord. Along-side my heart beat came the word ponder, it echoed until my heart was still. I saw before my heart's eyes lose strings. The strings were different in colour, shape and size. The only common thing about them is that they are strings. The strings came alive and began to dance. I tried to ignore them but they would not go away. I let them be and watched as if watching a film. In this case, the film was inside of me. The strings began to intertwine and began to weave themselves into a beautiful mat. They rippled against each other and created a beautiful harmony, following a rhythm I could not hear. Their colour sparkled and the strings radiate joy. I could feel this joy and my heart began to dance. As I watched, it became clear to me that we are uniquely and beautifully made. When we are alone our beauty seem useless, but together we give a clearer picture of God's plan for our world. We must remain uniquely different but in communion. As I pondered I felt a strong call to go share God's love to people everywhere. This sense of peace I feel within, I try to communicate to all around.

MAY 2002

VISION

The night is cool the stars are bright I sat on a stone, leaned against a hedge and began to pray. I found myself in a dark space. Gradually the darkness became clear. I was standing at the edge of two roads, one on the right and the other on the left. The road on the left was wide, smooth and full of people there where light in the shops and I could hear music from the surrounding. The road was filled with activity. I stood starring at the road. It looked like a massive shopping centre.

An old woman drew my attention to the road on my right. It was narrow with lots of potholes. The old woman sat at the entrance of the road she beckon me closer. As I came closer to her she said, very few people pass though this road and most of them turn back and join the other road. I decided to pass through the road. The right side of it was like a forest full of dead plants. Every tree or grass was dead. On the left there was a big space that prevented one from crossing to the other road. I kept looking at all that was happening on the other road. I decided to turn back and go into the other road, but a pink rose flower in the midst of all the dead plants on the right caught my attention.

The rose flower was as bright as light and was so beautiful. It stood out within the dead plants. I went towards the flower to pluck it, but it seems to move away from me. The closer I went the further it moved. I kept following the flower entranced by it beauty. As I went farther into the road the rose flower disappeared. I noticed then that I have lost sight of the other road. I began to search for the rose flower going further into the road. Something drew my attention upward and I saw a dot of light in the sky. As I stared, it drew nearer and brighter. The light became so large and as bright as the sun. Straight lines made of light grew out of the four corners of the light to form a cross. Unlike the sun, I was able to look directly at the light without hurting my eyes. The giant cross rested on the ground in front of me. From behind it a man in white came out. He told me to follow him. As I went behind the cross, the man disappeared.

Behind the cross I saw an open space with a door-like shape leading into the cross, I stepped in. I found myself in a beautiful garden. It cannot be compared to any garden on earth. Every flower is three times bigger than normal. A stream runs through the garden. The water was as clear as crystal. In the middle of this beautiful garden, I found the man I was looking for. He smiled at me and took me around the garden. He explained that the water give life to all the plants. As I looked at the top of the garden, all the flowers and plants form a lovely mass of colours. Each flower has a unique beauty yet blends in harmony, as I stared at the garden in wonder. The man said to me, the plants are all connected. I stood starring at this beautiful garden, and then I became aware of the fact that we are all interconnected and together we reflect the essence of creation. I felt so happy and so at peace. I wanted to stay in this garden forever. I felt the man, the garden and I are one. As I stared at the beautiful garden, I became conscious again of the bright stars, the cool night and the hedge pressing against my skin.

PASSION

My heart is filled with longing. I have encounter love and have lost myself. I am ready to surrender to the core of my being. Instinctively I knew what to do. I must break with my past, forget my fears and live in the present moment. I have broken the chains of attachment and must sought the lover I long for in the one whose eyes are filled with tears, in the heart that bleed and in the stray forgotten and lonely. I have died to myself now I live only for you; Lover of my being. This is our Secret, our Passion and Silence.

I sat to pray there was silence; no words were spoken. There was emptiness a darkness that had stay with me for months. I had become comfortable with this silence; I remind still. I found myself in a space. There was a building made of cloud. When I walked into what seemed like a door, I found myself in a room that has no roof. A light shone down into the room from a single source everyone was sitting down, but I was standing by the doorway. There was an empty space with my name on it. In front of the room a man in white was speaking to the group, but I could not understand what he was saying. This experience happened over a period of time. One day I saw myself sited on the empty chair listening to what the man was saying and I could understand. Then the scene faded away and I returned to my prayer position. I tried to remember what was said, but I could not. I was filled with so much love. After that, I never had this experience again.

CALLED BY NAME

I sat in my room to pray. I was surrounded by silence then I began to fall into a deep hole. I found myself in a forest running up a high mountain. A gentle vibrant voice called my name. The sound rippled through my being. I ran up the mountain following the direction of the voice. It called again as I hesitated and I began to run.

I am lured to give up everything and live for love alone
Let go of everything and be with love alone
The world a distraction that pricks the heart to groan
The poor cry and I hear their voices prove
The weak stretched and touch my heart in love
I am spilt in two, feel apart yet a part

I am filled with love that burst into tears of awe
Today my lover is silent but lots are spoken in touch
My lover remains still yet rocks my being to passion
The world is still, locked to the fondle
that ripples my heart to groan
Feelings are lost, found in the fondle that
rocks my heart with passion

Oh God you kissed me in the breeze that caresses my skin
Your whisper of love tickles my heart as birds whistle their song
I am weak with passion drenched in
love I surrender to your grip
My heart long for mundane practices to flee and free my being
The pain increase the passion within burn unceasingly ablaze
Speechless my heart speaks in love, thankful for the pain

ALONENESS

Alone in the world filled with beauty
Restlessly I walked within the garden
Love in a mist embraces all around
In this garden filled with beauty
I heard the whispers of love in the air.

Alone with the beauty within this garden
I need companion it seems a pair
Love reflects around this garden
Love is felt deep and laden
Why this passion that burns within

Compelled to silence I am consumed in flames
Walking in love in this garden of fame
The wind glides softly across my face
God loves you it tickles with play
Consumed by love he died to save

I sit I stand restlessly I sway
Ablaze with passion that cradled to daze
I ate I drank nothing can ease
Love encircled in gentleness seize
Without your love life must cease

I am filled with love lured by its claim
Free at last flying I can pray
Drawn to places without words to maim
Purified by love I am filled with peace
Thank you God for life reclaimed.

I sense an oral that frightens my soul
A glimpse of eternity that fills with awe
I feel so watched lifted from all
A sense of protection that dares the foul

Someone is watching, I trembled in fear
Yet my fear dances with dare
All meaning is lost except in care
My pulse a symphony unknown and bare
My heart dances against my breast

I am lured into life's depth so dense
Filled with love fear loses its sense
Embraced by you, passion has sense
Ah! Love tickles expanding my fence

Mundane concerns chuckle and flew
Creation significant, different and new
Love! Oh Love, I feel your clue
How can I declare your passion anew?

My heart beats like the thumping of drum
My pulse dances like the surging of wave
Though I feel strong in weakness I slump
I surrender speechlessly yet I am warm
This passion a cradle has rocked me to being.

I am soaked in love, sucked in space
Drawn to a place of longing and waiting
I am crippled by love and pain of passion
I am sucked in space, surrounded by darkness

I am sliding fast into the depth of nothingness
Searching for an anchor to rest my soul
The anchor you are, I am fixed on you
Sliding too fast as love attracts my soul
In this void of nothingness, I am left asunder
In this void of peace I am left in wonder
In the awe of plunder my heart in wonder

To surrender emptiness, to attach a pain
To let go nothingness to attach is thorn
Striving in love too afraid to plunder

To wait is love; stillness is trust
Love must suffer for love to live
Love must wait for passion to stir
Waiting a potion that charms to love
Waiting a mirror, a reflection of trust
Ah! Waiting labours and Love is born

A veil conceal that which eyes cannot see
Behind the veil my sight is blind
As I wait patiently for the veil to dance out of sight
I began to learn the uneasiness of the unknown
My heart cries my soul yearns
Yet in contentment I wait with conviction in my heart
Love would find me again.

As I wait longingly. Nothing matters anymore
I am tickled with love my heart burns with longing
Before the veil my heart begins to see
Rituals, rites, words all unit into nothingness

My heart and focus is only on my lover
I move like a bird scourging though the skies
Making love with the wind and the sky
I am swimming in a pool of passion
I screamed yet my mouth utters no word

In this ocean of passion I row in a boat of love
My heart cries yet my being laughs
Encircled in this ocean of passion, all opposites units
I remain speechless for words have become a stranger.

I trust you God
It's just so hard for me to know what to do
I love you God
It's just so hard for me to understand
Love drives out fear

I look around me and I see your love and
I feel the love you have for me
But when I sit to pray nothing confronts
And I wonder what I can do
Am just so weak, I wait for you
But waiting seems so long. (Chorus)

I just can't understand
When I wait for you
The world is passing by
I want to hold you close
Just need to feel your arms
I fall to tear; I leap with joy
I just don't know where to start
My life is hard/ my life is filled
But when I look to you the silence fills the world
But I know you are there
I can feel your touch; I can feel your love
And I feel I am squashed with love
You cradle me and you make love to me

I trust you God, I know you know
I just don't know what to do
I trust you God, I know you know
I just don't understand love drives out fear
I trust you God and I know you're there
I just don't know what it means
Love drives out fear

In the wind that wheezes across my face
My lover kisses me
In the water that crease my skin
My lover makes love to me
I inhale the fragrance, drunk in the potion of love
My lover's stroke lit a fire in my heart
My head dances with my heart
My soul screams for joy
Every part of my being dance in love
I am free from the imprisonment of my ego
I've tasted love and close doors to my doubts. So (Ch)

BELOVED CELIBATE

Who says lovers must find a time to caress
That lovers have a season to love
I am the beloved celibate I am loved eternally
In the wind that caresses my face my
lover kisses me passionately
In the water that caresses my skin my lover makes love to me
I inhale the fragrance, drunk in the ecstasy of love
My head dances in harmony with my heart
My soul screams in ecstasy
I have become inseparable from my lover.

Can a locked door impede the freedom of love?
I am free from the imprisonment of my ego
I tasted the bliss of eternity and the door of language is closed
Lost in the wilderness of solitude, love unites my body and soul
In darkness I can see with closed eyes for my soul is limitless
In the drunkenness of love I dance like the eagle in the sky
My passion devours the wind and the stars
I have encountered the core of my being
I am free as the wind incapable of being hurt
In the freedom of love, I walked through closed doors
In the freedom of soul, I broke through
the imprisonment of my ego.

In my lover's arms, I stand alone yet not alone
Passion affects my sense I am incapable of thoughts
Oh! Sweet bitterness, beauty that prickles
Because of your love I have lost myself
Because the earth is your word, I have become a listener
The earth is a reflection of your face
You touched me and fondle every part of my being

I am on fire with your touch. In your love I am speechless,
Drawn into a space where lover and beloved are one
At the thought of you, my heart sings a thousand tunes
My pulse explodes within me in passion
In your love all opposites unite, sin becomes sinless
Past, present and future becomes inseparable
I am mad with passion, my cries of ecstasy music to your ears.

Who dares to go out searching for my lover?
My lover is found in creation the river of life
My lover stares in the heart that cares
My lover stares in arms out stretched for love
In the hearts that bleeds in the eyes of tears
Come away from the desert; my lover is near
Though my lover holds all, my lover's eyes my pearl
My lover's eyes a thousand colours merge as one
Ha! Who says lovers have a season to love
I am the beloved celibate; I say love is timeless.

LOVE RETURNS

Love in dialogue seeks the world
Can its light dispel the darkness in the world?
Can the warmth of love melt this frozen world?

Love burst forth and the earth trembled
Sin shuttles to flight
Love in might, hidden in the simple
Yet it beats mightily to sight

Love burst forth and the earth trembled
Its ray reflects on all around
Then love mightily pieced beneath
Transformed the depth frozen with fright
Within the depth love units all

It is in love all is made
Love has returned to claim the lost
I fell on my kneels that I may love
Love smiled, but I am in you
From within love burst forth and my body trembled
Sighted with fright, oh help I am swallowed alive
Then the heart through night regains its sights.

Love in might is born again
Love lit a fire in my heart and words girdled to flight
In love opposites unit
Oh love overwhelmed my heart insane.

LOVE IS

As I walked in the garden, I was filled with so much joy and at one with the trees, the birds and the wind. Ah! The earth moves with single rhythm and dances to a single tune. The birds, tree, breeze and I are one. I could hear the birds, trees and breeze and understood their language of love. Ah love surrounds us, beautiful, wonderful and gloriously joyous. In the middle of this garden God is present, loving this world to being. Oh what a sight, what fragrance, what passion, what presence is this. How does one describe such beauty, such wonder and such wholeness? All reflect love and there is good in all things. This is beyond words in wonder I remain silent.

WAITING

Darkness lures the heart to wait
Radiant with light the tingling sun
Lures awake the calming dawn
To break from night the planet's run
A dot of light dances to sight
The light dances gently around
Imprisoned by light, power is powerless

Overwhelmed with sadness that dances with joy
Powerless to act waiting a tool
My heart longs for the feel of something
Tears roll like heavy rain drops
It's strange to cry the tears of nothing
Stretch like death the ground is formless

The force of love cripples my ego
I am only human with a taste of bliss
Driven and lost in the land of feelings
Words are dumb in this bliss of love
The tick of time is leech to the moment
Words are dumb to the lover's tale

Numb to words love is born
My unworthiness pops giddily to sight
My sinfulness battles fatally for might
Numb to speak, lots were spoken
In the sound of silence a burst of fright
Save me love, less I perish
In this silence of void time is timeless
In this ripple of love darkness is light
Overwhelmed with passion crippled to act
In this void of love sin is sinless.

INTIMACY WITH THE DIVINE

The earth is infused in love
I feel its warmth in the depth of my being
It calms the chaos within
I am soaked in love, drenched by its passion
You kissed and fondle every part of my being

In the breeze that wheezes across my face you kissed me
In the water that caresses my skin you made love to me
I am powerless to resist these blessings
You are the reason for the reasons

What fragrance what beauty what madness?
I am intoxicated with passion
I have lost myself in this present moment
You are the pulse that beats within
The life of my being
I am encircled in your love and free only within your love

SURRENDER

I'm lured to give up everything and live for you alone
Let go of everything and be with your alone
The world a distraction that pricks the heart to groan
The poor cry and I hear their voices prove
The weak stretched and touch my heart in love
I'm spilt in two feel apart yet a part I'm drawn

I am filled with love that burst into tears of awe
Today my lover is silent but lots are spoken in touch
My lover remains still yet rocks my being with passion
The world is still locked to the fondle
that ripples my heart to groan
Feelings are lost, found in the fondle that
rocks my heart with passion

Oh God you kissed me in the breeze that creases my skin
Your whisper of love tickles my heart as birds whistle their sing
My heart long for mundane practices to flee and free my being
The pain increase the passion within burn unceasingly ablaze
Speechless my heart speaks in love, thankful for the pain.

Where goes love when lovers caress
Rolling in seasons while boundary sway
I am the lover sealed by timeless sway
The wind of silence the kiss of passion
The rain a fondle that ripples the heart
The stroke of love channels the heart

Love issues forth from the cradle of heart
In the wonder of love the heart is silent
Words a flame lures the hand to write
In the bed of sheets words began to dance
Eyes are blind but sighted with passion
Words are dumb that freeze the lover's tale.

Nothing matters anymore
Mundane concerns passes like the wind
I feel alone yet surrounded by love
The dislikes of some pierce my heart to bleed
Yet love respond to hate with love

They plot against me to put me to shame
Their words and actions chuckled to lame
To be bruised is good for the sake of love
Oh sweet bitterness, my heart proclaims
To stay on earth a shuttle of pain

Pain pierced my heart and my body to action
Oh! The earth has become a distraction
I long to merge, to depart from here
Yet, I cannot people need my glare
Enfold in your love reclaim my love

Is love the rose and its thorn that pricks in sneer?
Like a broken pipe the tears rolled heartily to merge
Love smears the glue an ardent zeal to merge
I am weak with the passion that fills my being
So in the house of love hatred is vain.

I became aware of fullness in my chest.
I felt choked, breathless
Something has taken over me
Some force is overpowering me
Something tickles my being to rest

Joy and sorrow dances in harmony
Something within burst into tears
The tears were flowing, but I was not crying
Words failed me; actions failed me too

I longed to reach out to gather people to my lover
Yet I sense people a distraction
The tears kept flowing but I was not crying
All thing merge as one in love
Alone, I see all things a reflection of love

I have become a stranger in this world
Oh I have lost my senses I feel so apart
A voice whispered into my heart
You are not apart, love bridges the gap.

I worked along the garden
My heart began a prayer
God is present here I ponder
As true as on the altar

Then my heart began to thunder
Talk to me! Talk to me!!
Talk to me I know your are nearer
Today we must be passionate together
Tomorrow we celebrate together

Please talk to me talk to me
I can hear your voice calling fonder
Your attention is solely dearer
Your closeness is warmly tender
I need love's passion lingering longer

I walk along the garden
My heart raised in praises
In the midst of the birds singing praises
A single bird called out in phrases

My heart leapt in wonder
God has called as lover
Walking the garden in prayer
God lifts off my burden.

EMPTINESS

Restlessly I wait as darkness encompass my soul
A cloud as dark as night encompasses my being
I am surrounded by emptiness nothing looms to light
My eyes are blind to see, for nothing seems in sight
My ears are deaf to hear, my heart tremble in fright

Surrounded by silence, I felt the emptiness of darkness
Surrounded by darkness I felt the uneasiness of the unknown.

In stillness I wait as tears roll down my check
Just darkness, deep darkness full of emptiness
Love dance longingly in my heart
As in the darkness beauty emerge
Yet in darkness I wait trusting the dance of love.

In the stupor of prayer I dance with time
From within heaven and earth a union ensure
A power is born and time endure
Into the depth from the solid ground
Emptiness ensue in the cloud of love

Love speaks a word strange it sound
Suspended in void, surrounded by love
Longing for clarity the beauty of words
Twisting my soul words recoiled and drowned
Wrapped in emptiness surrounded by love
The pain of sin flew in like a dove
Though the self is lost the soul resounds

The pain of longing pricked my soul
A wave of silence tickled my soul
Expel my falsehood till falsehood is lost
Expel my sin till sin is lost
Hold on to me till I am held in love

In this darkness of void love resound
I wait till waiting ease it ground
Time drowned in grief recoiled to a mound
The words within are lost to sound
Yet in the depth of the void fear is fearless.

Deep in darkness, night began to play
Waiting for something in this land of nothing
I travelled in prayer to a space of nothing
My heart the beat and trees the song
Heart bleeds with love, trees sway with joy
I listened in awe the trees are singing.

My heart is tickled, tears my vault
The tree a cradle embraces my soul
The tree a cradle that rocks my soul
Creation sings and dances as one
The birds whistled, making love to a tree

Sprout to life the pulsing of music
Love the trees making the music
The tree a cradle that rocks my soul
Making love to the trees, God surely is here
Overwhelmed with love tears a stranger

The eyes of passion love to spare
The trees and I in union we share
The wind of love cradles the world
With wonder I slumped in gratitude to thee
The Divine climate embraces in love
Here love ripples generous to share.

My lover bright and radiant holds on to me
I have seen your face, my sight is blind
I have tasted your goodness, all else is tasteless
I tremble as my senses respond to thee
Your fragrance rouses me to new heights
Held in bliss the world no longer lives

Leeched to you, life must cease
In union with you, life increase
The past and future unite as one
Deaf to all, I cease to hear
Oh! Lover, take me with you

Gently in love my lover laughs
You are my presence the world can see
Longing for me your life must be
You in bliss that bliss descends

Go from me to stay with me
Held in love my soul in tears
My being quiver, dances in love
Grateful to this lover that loves me to birth

Tears... Tears.....Tears!!!
Love tickles my soul and life dances in my core
Driven and lost in the land of feelings
Words are dumb in the bliss of feelings
Words are dumb to tell the lover's tale
The veil of clarity is drawn to sail

I in God and God in me
This dance of love tickles my soul
Overpowered by love I yield to peace
The force of love crippled my ego
I am only human with a taste of bliss
The tick of time is leeched and ceased

Like a corpse I lie in stillness
Like death I am drained of life
Tears, tears as stillness embraced my soul
Ah! I am nothing all I am is you.

DIVINE CONNECTION

Who says lovers must find a time to cares;
that lovers have a season to love
Mine is the eminent lover, I am loved eternally
In the wind that wheezes across my face
my lover passionately kisses me
In the water that caresses my skin
my lover makes love to me
I inhale the fragrance drunk in the ecstasy of love
My lover's fondle lit a fire in my heart
My head dances in harmony with my heart.

I have become inseparable from my lover
I have tasted the bliss of eternity the door of language is closed
In the dark I see with closed eyes for my soul is limitless
I have encountered the core of my being; I am the spirit of love
In the drunkenness of love, I dance like an eagle in the sky
My passion devours the wind and the stars
I am lost in the wilderness of feelings

Can a locked door impede the freedom of love?
In the freedom of love, I walk through closed doors
In the freedom of soul, I broke through the constraint of ego
I am free from the imprisonment of my ego
I am free as the wind incapable of being hurt
I have come in contact with immortality

I have become a stranger to myself
In my lover's arms, I stand alone yet not alone
Passion affects my senses, I am incapable of thinking
Oh! Sweet bitterness, beauty of thorns
Come away from the desert, my lover is here

You hold all, yet your eyes rest on me
The earth is you word, I have become a listener
The earth a mirror that reflects your face
In your love my heart sees uncountable beauty
I can no longer see that which is not you
Your touch fondles every part of my being
Your love ripples and my heart a thousand tunes
My pulse explodes within, I have lost myself;
my cries of ecstasy music to your ears

In your love all opposites unit; sin becomes sinless
Past, present and future fuse as one
Your eyes a thousand colours merge as one
Ha! Who says lovers have a season to love
Mine is the eminent lover; I say love is timeless.

✎ CONCLUSION ✎

Prayer is a door into silence where God may speak. It is being present to the God who is always present to his creature. Let us look at different aspects of prayer as the bible says it.

Jer. 29:12-14. The Lord says, "You will call to me, you will pray to me....with all your heart and I will answer you..... So prayer is vocal, and in Ps. 25:1 it is calling on God and telling him what we need in our distress. Is. 55:6-9 says but we must first forsake our wicked ways and our evil thoughts.

Jer. 29:14 says, '... You will seek me with all you hearts and you will find me'. In Dt. 4:29-34 The word of God says, "Seek the Lord with all your heart and soul when you are in distress and you will find him. The prophet Isaiah says seek the Lord while he may be found. This kind of seeking involves mindfulness; being present to God and seeking him in our day to day activities.

Mindfulness is focusing on where I am who I am with and what I am doing at the present moment. This involves doing one thing at a time; being present to the present moment. Meeting with the God who says I am not I was.

Sometimes we focus too much on the past what could have been; who we could have met. Or we focus on the future where we are going; the job we would do; the course we would study; most of the time we miss the joy of the present moment. Who am I with now? How can I make the best of the present moment? How can I improve my life now? You must understand that the past is gone, the future does not exist and may never come; the present is all you have and you must make the best of it. To seek God is to search for God now. In Ps. 46:10 the word of God says, "Be still and know that I am God". This stillness is so that we will be open and available to God. To know God is to develop a relationship with God. When you are present to what you are doing you will see, taste and experience God in that thing. Mother Mary Aikenhead the founder of the Religious Sisters of Charity advice her sisters to give full time to everything, even to the boiling of an egg. That is a profound insight; you become aware of God in every event and action. This is what it means to pray always; that all your action is charged with an awareness of God; my friend you are praying.

In Ps. 63:1 and Ps. 42:1 Prayer is longing for God. The psalmist say for you oh Lord my soul in stillness waits truly my hope is in you. So in prayer we long for God; wait for God; and hope in God. In this type of prayer we say nothing and we do nothing. In fact we do not have anything to say, we just sit in God's presence and long for God and desire his presence lovingly. We become still and silent so that we can tune into the Divine frequency which is always current. Then we are surrounded by the spiral of God's presence which overwhelms us and takes over and the spirit of God groans in us. Then we will truly experience our humanity undistorted moulded in love and infused in Love (God).

In Ps. 63:4-5 Prayer is lifting up our hands and heart in praise and thanksgiving to God. It is the Spirit of God groaning in us, when we do not know how to pray. God who understands all hears the voice of the spirit in us Rom. 8:26-27.

I hope this Journal has brought you to a space where prayer is experienced as love relationship and God is experienced as always present.